A Father's Heart

BY THOMAS KINKADE

Copyright ©1998 by Thomas Kinkade, Media Arts Group, Inc.

All works of art reproduced in this book are copyrighted by Thomas Kinkade and may not be copied or reproduced without the artist's permission. For information regarding Thomas Kinkade art prints, collectibles and other products, please contact:

MEDIA ARTS GROUP, INC.
521 Charcot Avenue
San Jose, CA 95131
1.800.366.3733

All rights reserved. No portion of this book may be reproduced in any form without the written permission of the Publisher.

Printed in Hong Kong

Design and production by: Lucy Brown Design, Santa Barbara, California

ISBN 0-9638635-9-2

THOMAS KINKADE
Painter of Light

*When we love something it is of value to us,
and when something is of value to us we spend time
with it, time enjoying it and time taking care of it.*

M. Scott Peck

It is the simple things that make living worth-while, the sweet fundamental things such as love and duty, work and rest and living close to nature.

LAURA INGALLS WILDER

Thomas
Kinkade

Home is where the heart is,
The soul's bright guiding star.
Home is where real love is,
Where our own dear ones are.
Home means someone waiting
To give a welcome smile.
Home means peace and joy and rest
And everything worthwhile.

ANONYMOUS

Picture a place you're yearning to be.
A place where work, home,
and play are properly balanced,
where people exist peaceably,
where relationships flourish.
A place where there's time for
what's really important.

THOMAS KINKADE

*Each life is a masterpiece in the making.
And if your perspective is true, the whole
canvas will be beautiful.*

THOMAS KINKADE

Thomas
Kinkade

Nothing I've ever done has given me more joys and rewards than being a father to my children.

BILL COSBY

You will find as you look back upon your life that the moments when you have really lived are the moments when you have done things in the spirit of love.

HENRY DRUMMOND

*K*eep true to the dreams of thy youth.

JOHANN VON SCHILLER

The real voyage of discovery consists not in seeking new landscapes but in having new eyes.

MARCEL PROUST

The best things you can give children,
next to good habits, are good memories.

SYDNEY J. HARRIS

*In everything set them an example
by doing what is good.*

TITUS 2:7

*A wise man has great power,
and a man of knowledge increases strength.*

PROVERBS 24:5

The more I study nature,
the more I am amazed at the Creator.

LOUIS PASTEUR

As the Father has loved me, so have I loved you. Now remain in my love.

I will instruct you and teach you in the way you should go; I will counsel you and watch over you.

PSALM 32:8

Thomas
Kinkade

*Impossibilities vanish when a man
and his God confront a mountain.*

ROBERT SCHULLER

Thomas
Kinkade

*The strength of a man consists in finding out
the way God is going, and going that way.*

HENRY WARD BEECHER

But if we walk in the light, as he is in the light, we have fellowship with one another.

1 JOHN 1:7

The heavens declare the glory of God:
the skies proclaim the work of His hands.
Day after day they pour forth speech:
night after night they display knowledge.

BOOK OF PSALMS

Something deep in our spirit makes us long to be out of doors, to be renewed in the presence of nature. If you listen, the world of sky and water and trees can teach you. It can change you. It can make your life profoundly simpler and more satisfying.

THOMAS KINKADE

Thomas Kinkade

Thomas Kinkade, "The Painter of Light", is one of America's most collected artists. In the tradition of the 19th century American Luminists, Kinkade uses light to create romantic worlds that invite us in and evoke a sense of peace. Kinkade paints a wide variety of subjects, including cozy cottages, rustic outdoor scenes, dramatic landscapes, and bustling cities. Each painting radiates with the "Kinkade glow" that he attributes to "soft edges, a warm palette, and an overall sense of light."

Thomas Kinkade is a messenger of simplicity and serenity in these fast-paced turbulent times. His paintings are more than art, they are silent messengers of hope and peace that lift our spirits and touch our hearts.

Thomas Kinkade was born in Sacramento, California in 1958, raised in humble surroundings in the nearby town of Placerville. Kinkade apprenticed under Glen Wessels, an influential artist who had retired in the community. He later attended the University of California and received formal training at Art Center College of Design in Pasadena.

As a young man, Thomas Kinkade earned his living as a painter, selling his originals in galleries around California. He married his childhood sweetheart, Nanette, in 1982, and two years later they began to publish his art. In 1989 Lightpost Publishing was formed.

Thomas Kinkade is a devout Christian and credits the Lord for both the ability and the inspiration to create his paintings. His goal as an artist is to touch people of all faiths, to bring peace and joy into their lives through the images he creates. The letters he receives everyday testify to the fact that he is, at least at some level, achieving this goal.

A devoted husband and doting father to their four little girls, Kinkade always hides the letter "N" in his paintings to pay tribute to his wife, Nanette, and the girls often find their names and images tucked into the corners of his works.

"As an artist I create paintings that bring to life my inspirational thoughts and feelings of love, family and faith. I hope each image in my collection acts as a messenger of hope, joy and peace to you and your family."

Welcome to the Thomas Kinkade Collectors' Society

Dear Collector,

Some painters would say that they work with pigment, others with color. I prefer to think that I paint with light. Surely, God paints His creation with light, and that inspires me. I hope you'll agree that there is a radiant quality to my paintings, as if it were lit from within.

That effect is something members of the Thomas Kinkade Collectors' Society especially enjoy. So when I invite you to join us, I'm really urging you to let your light shine. With the help of Collectors' Society members, we'll illuminate a world of beauty and grace this year.

By joining the Thomas Kinkade Collectors' Society, you will enter a world of beauty that only Thomas Kinkade can create. Your membership for 1998 will include a very special "Welcome Kit" and members-only benefits to last all year long. For information on how you can join the Thomas Kinkade Collectors' Society visit your local Authorized Dealer or call: 1 . 800 . 544 . 4890

Visit our Website at:
www.thomaskinkade.com

1998 offers available
January 1, 1998 - December 31, 1998

INDEX OF WORKS